365
Powerful
Affirmations

FOR BLACK MEN, WOMEN, AND CHILDREN

Erin Francis-Malloy

365 Powerful Affirmations for Black Men, Women, and Children by Erin Francis-Malloy

First Printing, 2025.

ISBN: 979-8-9927401-0-3

Cover Design by Erin Francis-Malloy

Francis-Malloy Press
3920 Lindell Blvd Suite 209 #1173
St. Louis, MO 63108

Printed in the United States of America

Erin Francis-Malloy

Affirmations: A Brief Primer

affirm (transitive verb): validate, confirm; to state positively; to assert (something, such as a judgment or decree) as valid or confirmed; to show or express a strong belief in or dedication to (something, such as an important idea)

affirmation (noun): the act of affirming; something affirmed; a positive assertion

Words, whether positive or negative, are regarded by many as influential on nearly everything—with positive words having a positive influence, and negative words having a negative influence. While the metaphysical mechanisms of words don't have much empirical support, the evidence for their neurological and psychological effects is growing. Affirmations are positive statements that can help people cope with or recover from negative situations, emotions, feelings, and thoughts.

Repeating a positive statement won't immediately change the things around you--according to neuroscientists, the change occurs internally. Changing thinking patterns or thoughts (such as from negative thinking to positive thinking) contributes to neuronal rewiring, which then impacts behaviors, feelings, mood, and motivation.

Affirmations affirm self-worth, and have been associated with improved well-being, academic performance, and stress reactivity—and increased activity in the brain's self-processing and valuation.

Some benefits of affirmations are that they:
- help reprogram the subconscious

- support the creation of a better picture of one's self and surroundings
- lower stress levels
- decrease anxiety, fear, sadness, and worry
- improve quality of life
- improve mood by promoting feelings of happiness and optimism
- build the habit/neuronal wiring for positive responses to challenging circumstances

Affirmations may be used anytime and anywhere. Some common ways to use affirmations include saying them aloud, saying them in the morning, saying them in front of a mirror, incorporating them in breathwork or meditation, or adding them to something you do regularly (e.g., showering, cleaning, drinking coffee, etc.), to create a ritual. It may be particularly useful for some people to discuss these and other affirmations with loved ones or friends.

Finally, positive statements are only the beginning. Your words must be followed and supported by action. I would also like to remind you that just as positive affirmations have the above positive benefits and impacts on the brain, negative thoughts can have negative effects on behavior, mood, and thoughts/beliefs. For those who practice a religion, remember what your religion teaches about the power of words. Choose wisely!

You likely have more to gain than lose by affirming yourself!

Given the benefits of affirmations, why did I write a year's worth of daily affirmations "for black men, women, and children?" Affirmations, including the ones in this book, may be used by anyone and everyone. But I wrote and curated these especially for black people because of the generations of negative thoughts and programming that black people have been subjected to. Everyone may not agree with or like this focus, understandably. I'll leave a more eloquent rationale, by Dr. Joy DeGruy, here for any additional explanation needed:

> *"What stands between a disrespected African-American and the source of disrespect is almost four hundred years of history, four centuries of being the targets of humiliation and abuse. A history of racial conflict, inequality, and contempt culminates in a moment that few people not of the culture could comprehend, let alone predict."*

Health & Wellness

"Caring for myself is not self-indulgence, it is self-preservation, and that is an act of political warfare."
–Mrs. Audre Lorde

I will allow myself to rest regularly and without guilt.

I am healthy.

I release those thoughts and things that no longer serve me.

I attend to my health holistically and seek holistic health care.

Positive thoughts help me become healthier.

I eat health-supporting foods.

I am in harmony with nature.

I am at peace.

Everything I do or say makes me healthier.

I am healthy and vibrant.

It's okay to take a break.

My habits are health-supporting.

I am balanced.

I am divinely guided.

I am one with the universe/Most High/my higher power, etc.

I am protected/divinely protected.

I am connected to the wisdom of the universe.

I am rooted to the earth. She supports and loves me.

I allow rest and luxury into my life.

I trust my intuition.

My energy is high, clean, and pure.

I embrace pleasure, abundance, and creativity.

I am divine.

I heal myself and others.

My sexuality is vibrant, healthy, and sacred.

My intuition is accurate and clear.

I am a spiritual being in a human body.

I honor the divine within me.

I am a reflection of God/the Most High/Source/etc.

I am made in God's image/the image of my higher power.

Managing my emotions will improve my quality of life.

Managing my emotions will improve my decision-making.

My relationship with my emotions is healthy.

I value and honor my emotions and feelings, and the purposes that they serve.

I acknowledge and express my emotions and feelings appropriately.

I think about how my actions will affect how I feel.

I elevate my emotions and mindfulness whenever I can.

I maintain awareness of my feelings.

I recognize emotional cues and changes in myself and others.

I am able to self-regulate my body, behavior, thoughts, and emotions.

I attract sacred or positive spiritual connections.

I am thriving in every way and in all that I do.

I attract high-vibrational energy and experiences.

My self-identity, self-worth, and self-concept are positive.

My self-esteem is high.

I attract and maintain good health.

I can and will create and enforce boundaries with my family members.

My mental health matters.

I listen to my gut feelings and honor them.

I am divinely designed.

My mental health is just as important as my physical health.

I manage and process my emotions effectively.

I let go of people, behaviors, and situations that don't elevate me and are not healthy for me.

I nourish myself with water, food, people, behaviors, and situations that elevate me and are healthy for me.

I attract and maintain spiritual health.

I am healed.

I am physically and mentally fit.

I am vibrant.

I am full of vigor and vitality.

I am open to receiving the support and guidance I need to heal.

I release what doesn't support my health and growth, and I welcome healing and transformation.

I discontinue and change unhealthy patterns in myself, my family, and my community.

I am open to healing and growth in all aspects of my life.

I don't blame myself for my childhood experiences.

I don't carry anyone else's stuff: I don't internalize hate, mediocrity, abuse or insecurity.

I create and maintain healthy patterns in myself, my family, and my community.

I know what my triggers are, and how to react to them appropriately.

Rest is productive, restorative, and required.

I prioritize my health and wellness every day.

Prosperity

"Saving builds security; investing builds fortune."
–Dr. Boyce Watkins

"Some people are so poor, all they have is money."
–Mr. Bob Marley

Money comes easily into my life.

Even if I didn't come from health and wealth, prosperity in health and wealth will come from me.

I am healthy, wealthy, and wise.

My life is getting better and better.

I have everything that I need.

I am proud of my growth.

I embody prosperity.

I can have everything I want in life.

I let go of negative experiences and thoughts.

My wealth and net worth are constantly increasing.

I have a healthy and positive relationship with money.

I have financial and time freedom.

Debt does not control me.

I release my negative thoughts and feelings about money.

I deserve the money I earn.

My income and revenue potential and streams have no limits.

My income, revenue, and net worth don't define me.

I spend money wisely.

Money comes easily to me from the right sources.

I am wealthy beyond money.

I am open to receiving all forms of wealth.

I am creating generational wealth.

My children will have more than I have.

I come from prosperity, and prosperity will come from me.

Everywhere I go, I prosper.

Goodness and mercy follow me.

I think and operate in abundance, not scarcity.

I attract abundance.

I attract prosperous connections.

I am surrounded by love, success, and abundance.

I am a magnet for love, joy, and abundance.

I attract lucrative connections.

I create and maintain generational wealth in myself, my family, and my community.

Excellence & Success

"The future belongs to those who prepare for it today."
–Mr. Malcolm X

I am destined for greatness.

I attract and exude excellence.

I am an efficient learner.

I am qualified.

I am determined.

Everything I need is within me. The support I receive or meet is a bonus.

I am confident and competent.

I am proud of what I am accomplishing.

My hard work pays off.

My skills are valuable.

I am amazing.

I am successful.

I surround myself with positive people from whom I can learn a lot.

I learn, grow, and succeed from my mistakes.

My potential for success is limitless.

I know exactly what I need to do to be successful.

I am talented.

I work in a job or business that I love.

I am committed to fulfilling my life's purpose.

Small steps are also progress.

I embody excellence in every way.

I create my own power.

I am doing an amazing job.

I am victorious.

I embody confidence.

I have unique gifts to share with others.

I accomplish anything I put my mind to.

I edify myself and others.

I learn from life's experiences.

I am gifted.

I am a leader.

I am unstoppable.

I am educated.

I am focused.

I am ambitious.

I am a problem-solver.

I am intelligent.

I am skilled.

I am proud of who I am.

I am proud of who I am becoming.

I inspire others.

I will not accept less than my best from myself or others.

I am assertive.

I embrace the greatness within me.

My life is driven by purpose.

I turn challenges and obstacles into opportunities.

I will continue to learn and grow.

I lead by positive example.

I operate outside of my comfort zone.

Ignorance is not an option. I obtain or ask for information when needed.

I meet and exceed my expectations.

I embrace success.

I believe in my dreams.

I will spend dedicated time developing myself.

I am dedicated to progress, not perfection.

I welcome and value challenges because they help me grow.

I am a winner.

I move with intention and purpose.

I am surrounded by people who support me and my goals.

As I become more successful, I help more people.

I embrace a clutter-free life.

I trust in my ability to navigate through difficult times.

I adapt and learn from my emotions.

I welcome the lessons my feelings provide.

I balance reason and emotion.

Love & Happiness

"Black love is black wealth." –Mrs. Nikki Giovanni

"Don't wait around for other people to be happy for you. Any happiness you get, you've got to make yourself."
–Ms. Alice Walker

"I have decided to stick with love. Hate is too great a burden to bear." –Rev. Dr. Martin Luther King, Jr.

Love heals and accomplishes what hate cannot.

I deserve and choose to be happy.

I am worthy of love.

I love myself.

I am surrounded by love and support.

I love, and am comfortable in, my own skin.

Joy fills me easily and consistently.

I maintain or search for joy to prevent life's bitterness from overwhelming me.

I forgive myself.

I accept myself.

I enjoy myself.

I care for myself.

I love myself.

I am kind and compassionate to myself.

I am loved and supported.

I love and support others.

I allow pleasure, sweetness, and sensuality into my life.

I welcome love with an open heart.

I deserve joy and happiness.

I am proud of myself.

I celebrate all that I am.

I am kind to myself and my development.

My heart is free from past hurt.

I have people who love and care for me.

I radiate joy and pride in my heritage and culture.

I attract happiness and joy.

I love who I am.

I love who I am becoming.

I attract unconditional love.

I embrace love.

I will be patient and love myself as I heal.

Respect

"We all require and want respect, man or woman, black or white. It's our basic human right." –Mrs. Aretha Franklin

"Bringing the gifts that my ancestors gave, I am the dream and the hope of the slave." –Dr. Maya Angelou

"I am somebody." –Rev. Dr. Jesse L. Jackson

I make my ancestors proud.

I am my ancestors' proudest dream.

I am worthy of good things.

I know my worth and remind others of theirs.

I deserve respect, protection, and nurturing.

I matter.

I am worthy of being heard.

I treat others the way I want to be treated.

I am a priority.

I am worthy of self-care.

I am worthy of respect.

My peace matters.

I value myself.

My voice matters.

My words matter.

I am handsome/beautiful.

My experiences and feelings are valid.

I am worthy.

I am wanted.

I am important.

I am compassionate.

I am valuable.

My feelings matter.

My opinions matter.

I am allowed to be myself.

Being myself is enough.

I am connected to the ancient wisdom of my ancestors.

I fight for myself and for others.

I am allowed to take up space.

My life matters.

My voice deserves to be heard.

I am worthy of love, compassion, and forgiveness.

I deserve to be successful.

I deserve to move through life with ease.

I am proud of my heritage and ancestors.

My heritage and ancestors are proud of me.

I will speak kinder, healthier, and wealthier to myself.

I will spend dedicated time caring for myself.

My elders, ancestors, and I are proud of my decisions and achievements.

I stand on my ancestors' shoulders.

I honor my elders and ancestors.

I am needed.

I am heard.

I am understood.

I deserve love, respect, and compassion from myself and others.

I allow myself to heal at my own pace and in my own way.

I am allowed to feel strong emotions.

Gratitude

"Gratitude places you in the energy field of plentitude."
–Rev. Dr. Michael B. Beckwith

I'm exactly where I'm supposed to be at this point in my life.

I am grateful for everyone and everything I have in my life.

The more I give, the more I receive.

I am blessed.

I appreciate my life.

I appreciate each unique part of myself, inside and out.

I am filled with peace and gratitude, no matter what is going on around me.

I'm thankful for everything, the good and the bad.

I appreciate the moments of joy, happiness, and laughter in my life.

I am thankful for everything that I have, and all the good things that are coming my way.

I appreciate the power of gratitude to shift my perspective, attitude, and altitude.

I am grateful for the guidance and wisdom of my inner voice.

I am grateful for the guidance, wisdom, and protection of a higher power.

I am thankful for the courage to take risks and try new things.

I love and appreciate my mind and my body.

I am grateful for my wisdom, kindness, courage and strength.

I appreciate the moments of connection and understanding with myself.

I am grateful for the power of positive thinking.

I am thankful for the moments of peace and calm in my life.

I am grateful for the opportunities to connect with others.

I am grateful for my strength and resilience.

I am thankful the power of forgiveness to heal and transform me.

I am grateful for my financial success.

I'm glad that I'm here.

I am grateful for my health and vitality.

I am grateful for all that I have, all that I am, all that I will give, and all that I will receive.

I am grateful for the unique qualities that make me who I am.

Accountability & Integrity

"The time is always right to do what is right."
–Rev. Dr. Martin Luther King, Jr.

I am in control of my emotions. My emotions do not control me.

I don't waste energy worrying about things I can't control. I control how I react to them.

I trust myself.

My actions align with my values.

Being honest frees me.

I believe in myself.

I do great things.

I am disciplined in every way, belief, and action.

I am kind.

I am honest.

I am virtuous.

I am helpful.

I have, and embody, integrity.

I am accountable.

I am a person of substance, dignity, and integrity.

I am responsible for my happiness and development.

I use my voice to speak up for myself and others.

I am responsible for my behavior.

I am responsible.

I am responsible for my health and healing.

I do not make excuses for myself.

I am trustworthy.

I keep my word.

I operate in decency and in order.

Before I act, I think about the consequences of my actions.

I think about how my actions will make other people feel.

I think, and plan, before I act.

I am the author of how I feel about and react to everything.

My actions, words, intentions, values, and purpose are aligned.

Erin Francis-Malloy

Power & Creativity

"The most common way people give up their power is by thinking they don't have any." –Ms. Alice Walker

"Being a black creative is a blessing."
–Ms. Kirsten Campbell, Roll Up and Paint

I am creating the life of my dreams.

I inhale power, and exhale peace.

My name is great.

I am capable.

I know myself.

I express myself.

I am creative and inspired.

I am empowered.

I say "period" because my affirmations aren't questions.

I feel comfortable speaking my mind.

I am powerful.

I am clear and concise.

My influence is positive and profound.

I empower myself and others.

I can manifest my intentions and vision.

I attract everything that I desire.

I can make a difference.

I attract clarity.

I am a powerful creator.

I create the life I desire.

I have the power to make my dreams a reality.

My powers to create and destroy are balanced.

Chakras & Energy

"We are all connected. To each other, biologically. To the earth, chemically. To the rest of the universe, atomically."
–Dr. Neil deGrasse Tyson

"You matter. Unless you multiply yourself by the speed of light squared. Then you energy." –Dr. Neil deGrasse Tyson

If you're not familiar with the concept of chakras, you may be wondering what they are? Conversely, if you're familiar with chakras, you may be wondering why I mentioned them? Well, to support them with affirmations, of course. If you're familiar with them, please skip ahead to "Root Chakra" for affirmations that aim to support each chakra.

In Indian yoga tradition, chakras refer to seven circular centers of energy throughout the body that allow energy to flow when they are "open." Blockages in any chakra are associated with functional or health problems where the chakra is located. From the top of the head to the base of the spine, the seven chakras (and the colors associated with them) are:

- the crown chakra, or Sahasrara (violet)
- the third eye chakra, or Ajna (indigo or purple)
- the throat chakra, or Vishuddha (blue)
- the heart chakra, or Anahata (green)
- the solar plexus/navel chakra, or Manipura (yellow)
- the sacral/pelvic chakra, or Svadhisthana (orange)
- the root chakra, or Muladhara (red)
-

For example, a blocked throat chakra may contribute to speech problems, feeling speechless or tongue-tied, talking too much, etc. The most common way to unblock chakras and support chakra health is the practice of yoga. It also may not hurt to speak life into your energy centers or even wear colors associated with a particular chakra.

Root chakra (associated with the pelvic floor/base, survival, and grounding):
- I am safe and secure
- I am grounded, centered, and safe.

Sacral chakra (associated with the sex organs, fertility, and creativity):
- I create my reality and cleanse my energy.

- I am creative and sensual.

Navel chakra (associated with digestion, personal power, and purpose):
- I am powerful and intelligent.

- I stand in my personal power.

Heart chakra (associated with compassion, love, and the soul):
- I am love.

- I give and receive love.

Throat chakra (associated with speech, hearing, metabolism, and truth):
- I speak clearly and powerfully.

- I speak my truth.

Third eye chakra (associated with intuition, sixth sense, and knowledge):

- I am intuitive.

- I see with clarity and wisdom.

Crown chakra (associated with enlightenment and spirituality):

- I am connected to, and guided by, the divine.

- I am connected to my higher self.

Grand Rising

"You may trod me in the very dirt/But still, like dust, I'll rise." –Dr. Maya Angelou

"The boundless capacity of the African-American spirit in this country to say 'Hallelujah, anyhow,' to use our joy as a weapon, to use our creativity as a weapon, to use our moral clarity and our deep experience as a weapon, not just to save black people, but to save all of these people." –Dr. Van Jones

I am enough.

I am beautiful inside and out.

I am constantly evolving.

"I never fail. I either win or I learn." –Madiba Nelson Mandela

I was born to do great things.

I am resilient.

I am courageous.*

Only I define who I am.

I am here for a reason.

I break generational curses.

I will not let society define who I am.

I am comfortable in my skin.

I am confident in my skin.

I will never quit.

I won't allow racism to distract me from my greatness.

I recognize rejection as protection and redirection.

I am evolving and growing stronger with each passing day.

I am resilient, adaptable, and capable of growth.

My resilience is unmatched and has no limits.

Resilience is in my DNA and has been shaped by my experiences.

I continue to rise. I am stronger than what was meant to destroy me.

I release the burdens passed down through generations and embrace healing.

I forgive myself and others, liberating myself from resentment.

Every day, I get better at managing my reactions to stress.

*Feel free to use the word "fearless" if preferred. I prefer "courage" because courage isn't always the absence of fear. Courage can also be action in spite of fear.

Hope

"Hold fast to dreams, for if dreams die, life is a broken-winged bird that cannot fly." –Mr. Langston Hughes

"All people of African descent, whether they live in North or South America, the Caribbean, or in any part of the world are Africans and belong to the African nation."
–Mr. Kwame Nkrumah

I am open to new adventures in life.

I'm open to life's opportunities.

There are wonderful things in my future.

I support the unity, safety, respect, education, spirituality, health, and wealth of black people.

42 Principles of Ma'at

The following are 42 ideals or principles that have been associated with Ma'at, the ancient Kemetic goddess of truth, justice, harmony, and balance. They're regarded as guides to a truthful, just, harmonious, and balanced way of life, and are included here as additional powerful affirmations.

I honor virtue.

I benefit with gratitude.

I am peaceful.

I respect the property of others.

I affirm that all life is sacred.

I give offerings that are genuine.

I live in truth

I regard all altars with respect.

I speak with sincerity.

I consume only my fair share.

I offer words of good intent.

I relate in peace.

I honor animals with reverence.

I can be trusted.

I care for the earth.

I keep my own counsel.

I speak positively of others.

I remain in balance with my emotions.

I am trustful in my relationships.

I hold purity in high esteem.

I spread joy.

I do the best I can.

I communicate with compassion.

I listen to opposing opinions.

I create harmony.

I invoke laughter.

I am open to love in various forms.

I am forgiving.

I am kind.

I act respectfully of others.

I am accepting.

I follow my inner guidance.

I converse with awareness.

I do good.

I give blessings.

I keep the waters pure.

I speak with good intent.

I praise the Goddess and the God.

I am humble.

I achieve with integrity.

I advance through my own abilities.

I embrace the All.

When You Pray, Move Your Feet

An extra, bonus affirmation: áṣẹ (also spelled "ashe," pronounced "ah-shay"): among the Yoruba-speaking people of West Africa and of the African Diaspora in the Americas and other places, a word that means "power," "authority," "command," "energy," or "life."

Words are powerful, and people of African descent are often perceived as uniquely powerful in metaphysical or spiritual ways that aren't fully understood. If you don't feel powerful, speak it into existence. If you do feel powerful, be and speak powerfully!

If you found value, joy, validation, confirmation, or other positive takeaways in this collection of affirmations, don't stop here. Continue to affirm yourself on a regular basis or as needed. Affirmations may be found everywhere, but it's my hope that these are especially poignant, relevant, and salient to you and the wider global community. There are so many more affirmations around. Explore them—and if you feel creative, write your own personal affirmations! Áṣẹ!

One Last Thought: An Afterword

When I first thought about writing a collection of affirmations, I almost didn't follow through with it. It seemed silly or unnecessary. (And it may be, for some people, lol) The potential seriousness of affirmations for some people came to mind while I wrote them down.

Can you imagine that entire ethnic groups, social classes, age groups, sexes, etc. were programmed to believe that their peace doesn't matter? Or that they're worthless, powerless, or a "nobody?" Can you imagine how some people's mood, behaviors, motivation, and feelings may change if they change their thoughts or mindsets? Okay, okay, I'll sign off, now. :-) Continue elevating!

References

Cascio, C. N., O'Donnell, M. B., Tinney, F. J., Lieberman, M. D., Taylor, S. E., Strecher, V. J. & Falk, E. B. (2016). Self-affirmation activates brain systems associated with self-related processing and reward and is reinforced by future orientation. *Social Cognitive and Affective Neuroscience, 11(4)*, 621–629. https://doi.org/10.1093/scan/nsv136

Irele, A. (2010). *The Oxford encyclopedia of African thought (Vol. 1)*. Oxford University Press.

Kemet Experience. (2019). *The 42 ideals of Ma'at.* Retrieved from https://www.kemetexperience.com/the-42-ideals-of-maat/

Merriam-Webster. (n.d.). Affirm. In *Merriam-Webster.com dictionary.* Retrieved from https://www.merriam-webster.com/dictionary/affirm

Merriam-Webster. (n.d.). Affirmation. In *Merriam-Webster.com dictionary*. Retrieved from https://www.merriam-webster.com/dictionary/affirmation

Old Dominion University. (2023). *The power of positive affirmations.* Retrieved from https://www.odu.edu/equity/civility-month/affirmations

Yoga Journal. (2025). *A beginner's guide to the chakras.* Retrieved from https://www.yogajournal.com/practice/yoga-sequences-level/beginners-guide-chakras/